FIGHTING BACK

FIGHTING BACK

*facing devastation
with courage*

MARY ELIZABETH LAFORET

TATE PUBLISHING & *Enterprises*

Fighting Back
Copyright © 2011 by Mary Elizabeth Laforet. All rights reserved.

No part of this publication may be reproduced, stored in a retrieval system or transmitted in any way by any means, electronic, mechanical, photocopy, recording or otherwise without the prior permission of the author except as provided by USA copyright law.

This book is designed to provide accurate and authoritative information with regard to the subject matter covered. This information is given with the understanding that neither the author nor Tate Publishing, LLC is engaged in rendering legal, professional advice. Since the details of your situation are fact dependent, you should additionally seek the services of a competent professional.

The opinions expressed by the author are not necessarily those of Tate Publishing, LLC.

Published by Tate Publishing & Enterprises, LLC
127 E. Trade Center Terrace | Mustang, Oklahoma 73064 USA
1.888.361.9473 | www.tatepublishing.com

Tate Publishing is committed to excellence in the publishing industry. The company reflects the philosophy established by the founders, based on Psalm 68:11,
"The Lord gave the word and great was the company of those who published it."

Book design copyright © 2011 by Tate Publishing, LLC. All rights reserved.
Cover design by Lauran Levy
Interior design by Joel Uber

Published in the United States of America

ISBN: 978-1-61739-774-5
1. Biography & Autobiography; Personal Memoirs
2. Health & Fitness; Healing
10.12.22

DEDICATION

To all who have been paralyzed—physically, emotionally, mentally, or spiritually—and have searched for a better life, this book is dedicated.

T o the athlete in all of us.

A special thanks to: My 2 favorite former Loon's stars Andrew Lambo and Kyle Russell;

All my editors in this work: Kathleen Knapp, Alexa Matthews and the Midland Writers Group of Natalie Tucker, Dwight E. Williams, Len Gorgol, Marion J. Newman, Connie Miskov, Amy Blubaugh, and Linda L. Helm; my parents, Dr. John Kowalczyk AND....

Anyone I've ever danced with.

INTRODUCTION

In 1975, I survived a traumatic brain injury. As a result, I entered the world of total disability. I was 15 at the time. It's true that I had youth on my side. It is also true that I never underwent any significant improvement to my condition until many years later when I began to challenge the environment I lived in. In 1975, so little was known about how to care for the survivors of such an injury that they died, were institutionalized, or were discharged and "managed by family." I was fortunate enough to have a wonderful supportive family, but there was very limited professional help.

In the summer of 2008, my mother sent me a book, *Build a Better Brain*, by Dr. Daniel Amen. I was pleasantly reminded by the details in the book that it was this author who had introduced himself to me back in 1978 at Oral Roberts University, where we both were studying. As an ORU student, standards required the student to earn a minimum of 40 aerobic points per week. In my quest to earn the points, I used to run around the outskirts of the ORU campus twice daily. Daniel Amen who was studying to be a doctor had noticed me running. It's interesting how the emotions and mind work. I had blocked all memory of this super-human effort from my mind. In fact I had honestly forgotten most of my college years until I read Dr. Amen's description of himself and his brother.

Dr. Amen's nephew, Andrew, had problems with aggression. I chuckled when I read his description of his questioning his nephew's medical condition and the prescribed treatment. Dr. Amen had difficulty getting his medical colleagues to make the correlation between Andrew's brain SPECT results and his unexplainable aggression. (A SPECT is an earlier version of a brain scan.) Dr. Amen instinctively knew that a prescription for drugs, which was the usual treatment for this condition, was incorrect. He had the wisdom to find a surgeon who would consider the tumor shown in the SPECT scan as abnormal and remove it. His book indeed sought to link brain SPECT findings with treatments.

Dr. Amen also made another valid point in his book about being grateful for everything. This is probably the main reason I am where I am today, standing and walking, instead of in a wheelchair or fighting unconditioned nerves to make my body respond. When running around the ORU campus, I used to be very grateful for not falling as much as I had in earlier high-school days.

I felt compelled to write Dr. Amen to let him know I consider it a tragedy that medicine takes such a hands-off approach to so many things. I also wrote that I felt more had to be done to help the disabled veterans with head trauma coming back from serving our country. I told him I remembered his introducing himself to me all those years ago. I was disappointed but not too surprised that I never heard back from him.

I had every intention of just forgetting my experience with head trauma but when I was visiting my parents for the holidays, I saw an article on the front page of the *Tampa Tribune*, picturing a discharged veteran in a wheelchair. I had recently seen a similar picture of myself as I was viewing some of my mother's scrapbooking work. This guy was obviously a victim when the brain is jostled inside the skull and in all likelihood could benefit from what I have to say... my advice would start out with "I've been there" and end with "I learned that God is very real. I called to him the first time when I was at the Rehabilitation hospital and he answered. I will be forever changed. I've learned you can't have sin(laziness, doubts or negativity) in one area of your life and expect victory in another. Subsequently I cringe when I see the world today and how people with this disability are treated. I wonder if I may make a few suggestions which might benefit the physical body because I think that is where it all begins. You will need your physical body to get the necessary emotions to get angry and fight." Treatment from professionals never led anywhere in terms of improving my condition; at least not until I realized that it was *all up to me.* A neurologist had told me this relatively early in my recovery, that no-one would ever be able to help me like me, but back then I did not yet understand. Now I do understand and looking back at those years, I see denial played a very big part in my life. The book *On Death and Dying* by Elizabeth Kuebler-Ross, helped me to define this phenomenon. The thing that had died was me! I was denying that it bothered me. It was these memories of my own trauma and the unfruitful ways suggested in therapy to cope which came flooding back and I decided then to write this book.

As I scurry to complete the exercise I hope can re-establish more nerves to my right arm, I'm reminded of the conversation I once had with that neurologist after a few years of struggling to cope with this condition. He had stated "You just don't get it. Nobody knows. Your recovery can go just as far as you want it to but I can't tell you how to do it." With dead certainty I can say he was right. Nobody that I've looked to for advice has ever known how to do it.

But I can also say because of a few simple truths that somebody did teach me, my life is so much easier. And with this new ease came an improved quality to my speaking, an increased clarity in my vision and an amplified appreciation of sound, largely because I accepted the devastation and learned how to make the most of what I do have. True strength comes when the body can resist itself. Stories of how I did this might help. Sharing what I so slowly and painfully learned may help others caught in similar circumstance because I'm convinced that approaching life after this kind of trauma with the current lack of knowledge leads to greater distress than is necessary.

Because President Obama has put head-injury at the top of his medical agenda, I wish to speak out about these truths hoping to better the lives of those living with this condition and for all those suffering any nerve disorder.

CHAPTER 1

Without pain, where would I be......... ....

The accident occurred after a post-hockey game party, with friends. As we were going home, snow fell. On the side of the road ahead was a car in the ditch. We decided to stop to help. After successfully helping these strangers our own car slipped into the same ditch. I positioned myself by the back tire of the car's driver side. As another car approached, the young, inexperienced driver panicked and lost control. The impact of her sliding two-ton vehicle struck and threw me head first into the car I was pushing and broke my right clavicle. I fell to the ground unconscious, bleeding from a gash to the head. One of my friends, John, stayed with me while the others sought help. It was at least half an hour before they successfully roused someone to give assistance.

The ambulance driver noted that I had no pulse and reported me as dead; thankfully, the Emergency Room doctors were able to resuscitate me. The call to my parents must have been shocking. They said "your daughter has been seriously injured." and to come quickly to sign the release forms for treatment. Since my mother was a nurse, she knew what that meant. (I could already be dead.) Upon their arrival, they asked for the parish priest to perform last rites.

After surgery I was moved to the Intensive Care Unit. Family, friends, neighbors and other classmates from my high school sophomore class all rallied around to help in any way possible. The ICU had rules regarding the number of visitors allowed at one time, but a steady stream of them came by. It was a lively New Year's Eve at the hospital that year.

My face had swollen to unrecognizable proportions, prompting my mother to tape my 10th grade picture to the bedpost so the doctors and nurses would see the person beneath the injured body. Doctors suggested playing music tapes and telling visitors to speak to me as if I were aware. My high school friends made a tape of well-wishes and our band leader for whom I had played the flute gave a recording of the high school marching band's fall performance. A few close friends were instructed to use a paintbrush to sooth my constantly jumping arms and legs.

After two weeks, the hospital personnel noticed enough progress to move me to a private room at the hospital. My eyes fluttered, trying to open. Exactly three weeks after the trauma, January 19, 1976, I opened my eyes to a very welcoming family. It was my dad's birthday.

As the preparations for my rehabilitation began, I feared becoming like my little brother. He had been born suffering a fragile X chromosome which meant he was mentally handicapped. I instinctively knew something was wrong and since John had never achieved more than a kindergartner's mentality perhaps this was what had happened to me. I also couldn't talk. The second concern my caregivers had was whether or not I would ever talk again. Being placed on a tilt table caused me to scream in extreme pain a garbled but understandable "Put this thing down", ending any speculations that I wouldn't speak. Learning bladder control was another pain that prompted awareness. The hospital had suggested inserting a permanent tube for this but my mother had rejected signing the papers for that surgery. I tried with great difficulty to learn to navigate a wheelchair. This task was almost impossible since my right arm moved only reflexively. Soon I was ready for the rehabilitation hospital in Detroit, where a spot was available later that month.

With much thought memories of the first day at Detroit Rehab can still be recalled. The staff set a tray full of food in front of me. I was hungry, but because I had been right handed before, my left hand was not accustomed to using silverware. Using the left hand with no silver, I wolfed down cereal with milk. Eating wasn't the only issue. I believed that I should be able to get out of the bed and sit on the chair next to it. With no working nervous system in my right side, my right leg immediately collapsed and I fell to the floor. Hospital personnel ran to my room to tie me to the bed. The first real problem was the denial inherent in coping that accompanies a head injury. I thought walking would magically return and would happen only if I were moving. No one could convince me otherwise. I must have had wings on my heart.

CHAPTER 2

There but for the grace.......

My parents would come to the rehabilitation hospital to visit me at night. My father would put the safety belt around my waist and "walk" me up and down the halls of the hospital. At that time both physical and occupational therapy rotated twice during the week and speech therapy was also twice a week. I must have been too young to listen and understand what my Physical Therapists had to say. They could not convince me of my lack of strength and the need for resistance. All I really remember outside of my non-compliant attitude of wanting only to walk was that I learned to use a cane and navigate myself getting into and out of a car. On April 16th, I was discharged, still unable to move without losing my balance. A quad-cane assisted me with movement in the house and a wheelchair was necessary if I were to go any appreciable distance. The social worker and the rehabilitation center's psychologist did their best to point out my new limitations but my house essentially remained unprepared for a person with such disability. I didn't care to think of myself as having special needs. I could take the stairs in my tri-level home and if the stairs were a challenge, I could always lean over on the wall so there was really no danger.

Later that summer I fell and broke my foot. That May, my mother and I had been at a weekend retreat given at Oral Roberts University. The school hosted these retreats to introduce students to the school in order to build up the student body. I remember being escorted everywhere in a wheelchair and feeling extremely frustrated with life. During a worship service, I was wheeled to the healing line and instructed to rise and walk across the stage. I did so. Then the wheel chair was moved to the other side of the stage so I could be safely transported back to my room. Then one night, after several months of living with extremely limited circumstance, my high school friend Shelly was hosting a pool party to celebrate the final day of school and I was ready to try my wings. I refused to bring the wheelchair to her party, as it embarrassed me, and I again collapsed.

After weeks of pain, I finally went to the Emergency Room for an x-ray. A small bone in the top of my right foot had broken. The cast for its' healing went up almost to my knee. Strangely enough, walking with the cast was easy and I did it every day…..practicing, practicing, and practicing. When it came off 4 weeks later walking was a breeze. The ER personnel commented on my improvement and said that it must have been the weight of the cast. On the final trip to outpatient services at the rehabilitation hospital my therapist was happy with how much

I had improved. So in my new reality my brain had slight recognition of my foot.

In this condition it is so easy to get in a rut and become accustomed to the present, especially when there is no recollection of the past. I didn't realize it then but one's body is incredibly adaptable. Muscles not normally used can compensate for those muscles which have been disabled by brain injury. My movement was very labored. My right arm was rigidly spastic. Yet I clung to the belief that if I didn't use it, I would lose it. I knew people who didn't move die early. I read a book by Norman Cousins, *Anatomy of An Illness.* Norman wrote it because he was told that he had little chance of surviving cancer. He developed a recovery program that incorporated megadoses of Vitamin C, a positive attitude, love, faith, hope, and laughter. I would have the same emotional toughness and try to do the same as he did. I wasn't aware that physical improvement was something possible or probable. However, I wasn't going to let that interfere with my life.

I attended marching band camp later that summer. The caring band director had said I could be in the band again even if it meant I could only be in the flag corps. I needed a doctor's release to go to the camp. My family physician laughed at my mother for wanting to send me to such a physically grueling week and refused to sign the release. Well, on hearing of this, I cried to my mother that no one should be able to tell me I couldn't try. We went to another doctor to sign it.

I remember visiting a physiologist later that fall. He had no idea what might help me but thought that maybe dancing would lead somewhere. I was really inspired by the dance teacher. Mrs. Baker had 4 children and she ran a few miles every day. Even though the dancing was unreasonably challenging, I wanted to run just like her. In the family room, I used to put music on and run in place. The running motion was impossible to do prior to breaking my foot but that cast had given me an edge. The ER Doctor who had attended my broken foot from the previous summer had told me to keep my foot up as much as possible while he was molding the cast. That slight effort and the subsequent practicing gave me slight control over that foot. I found new determination. Eventually, I found with total concentration an abbreviated bearing of my weight by the legs made a scuttle possible.

On Easter day of 1977, I began to run on the roads of my neighborhood. During my first attempts, I fell often but the activity was a wonderful release. The endorphins produced gave me control over my emotions, so it was worth the occasional bloody knee or elbow. The unequal muscle imbalance in my legs led to injury and my hamstring and quadriceps tore often . Concentration over the placement of my right foot preoccupied my thought life, much to the detriment of my learning social skills. In my deepest heart, I knew I must look awkward but then I told myself as long as I was moving, strength would eventually return. Every time I caught a glimpse of myself, be it in a photograph or a reflection in a window I was passing, it made me want to stand straighter, concentrate more and work harder. I basically lived self-delusion. I dared not let my mind remember how effortless life had been prior to my injury. I had done cheerleading, dances at the previous year's talent show and skiing. Plus I had been on the swim team. I missed it.

Learning had become a greater challenge as I struggled with a tape recorder for taking notes. It was bulky until I got a pocket version several years later. I was only an amateur at best when recording and the sound of the voice only rang through clearly about 50% of the time. Hearing the same lecture twice did help, but not to the level I wanted. Plus I would need twice as much time to learn half the information. I graduated, however, 20th in GPA from high school. I received a standing ovation as I grabbed my diploma and crossed the stage at Ford Auditorium. My class standing must have been from the all-A status achieved prior to the injury, because my memory had become like a sieve and seemed to hold nothing.

Moving onto college, I went to Oral Roberts University. That weekend a few years prior convinced me I liked that school's spirit. I still used the tape recorder for notes and continued to run every day, logging four to ten miles daily. My arm was a useless appendage. I remember trying to swing it as I ran but that extra concentration caused me to trip, subsequently, I rarely did it. I recall someone remarking at the college cafeteria that my ability to eat with one hand was truly amazing. At the time I was offended but I learned that stares and comments were a prompt, reminding me of what appeared awkward to others; something which I might want to modify.

Almost super-human effort was required for just about everything as my resting heart rate was a mere 40 beats per minute. Doctors were telling me I had achieved 90% recovery yet I still felt so crippled. I was sad deep inside though my exterior portrayed differently. I always tried to appear cheerful. I used to stare almost neurotically at my leg. My father used to tease me desiring me to make light of it. I remember thinking and even verbalizing how people take so much for granted.

After two years, I left ORU to pursue a career not offered by the school. The summer before beginning my studies at Michigan State was eventful as I first began to use weights. My mother enlisted a personal trainer for me and I could do none of the weights in his gym on my own. At MSU, I remember continuing to attract stares. I remember going to a sports clinic because I had again torn my hamstring. After feeling my leg, the Doctor looked with fear in his eyes and commented, "You've been running like this?" and "Nobody ever told you about using weights?" I started using 2 pound ankle weights. At MSU, my roommate offered advice which I took to heart. She said I should listen to the authorities. So struggle to use the weights I did. While sitting on the floor and putting the ankle weight on my right leg I lifted it as far as possible. Agility did improve as some muscles regained ease in movement with the resistance. My heart rate never again achieved its 40 beats per minute status. Everyone seemed to notice. My counselor at Human Ecology was so impressed she suggested a scholarship in my name being established for the student who wanted to overcome insurmountable odds. The school turned her suggestion down citing that everyone has difficulties in life.

After graduating from college, I learned that head injury was becoming a more studied condition. The books I read said the sufferer felt isolated and denial was almost always a factor. I really didn't understand what denial was. Other tests done at an evaluation showed suicidal thoughts were present. Consequently, these results caused enough alarm to justify more treatments. Cognitive training on the computer suggested by the speech therapist improved my memory. A psychologist, Russ Reeves, named my condition *devastation*. He said that when I could face the devastation, I would then be able to choose whether I would accept it or beat it. He did not offer me false hope. My destination would be greatly influenced by my injuries. The cognitive therapy of writing everything I did and ate down helped me somewhat to control my emotional outbursts. The running I had been doing left me thinking I could eat whatever I wanted, giving no thought to what or whose food it was that I was eating. I remember my college roommate being abhorred by the behavior.

Another of Russ's suggestions was to get out on my own, so in 1984 I moved to Los Angeles to be near my friend Shelly. My mother, who had started a nursing pool just days before my injury in 1975, was by now an established "Woman Business Owner", even to the point of achieving an award in the White House. She had Business friends everywhere. I left to live with one of those friends and her family. This lady, also owned a temporary employment pool, so she had connections. Proving to employers I could be a valuable employee was a challenge. My walking resembled someone failing a sobriety test. I had difficulty typing. I had taken a typing class in 9th grade and done very well by reaching 40 words per minute so I knew how to type. But now that unconditioned nerve impulses traveled through my fingers and my arm preferred to cling to my side, I was lucky to achieve 10 wpm. Any faster meant more errors accompanied my work. Eventually I was hired as a file clerk. I stopped my daily running routine as it was too difficult in the city and the leg injuries interrupted my ability to work, so I opted instead to join the local YMCA. My degree meant nothing. Most food service positions required more physical agility than I had at that time.

CHAPTER 3

"I figured it out, what I needed was for someone to show me…"

Air Supply, "Lost in your love"

In 1985 I moved again to Philadelphia, after learning of Para-legal school which would help place me in better employment after achieving their certificate. As was promised, the certificate in corporate finance/business law landed me a job at a major bank doing loan documentation.

It was May of 1988 at the YMCA when a karate instructor took me aside and said to do a one-legged squat. He demonstrated and then said to do it 100 times, every morning. He said I could hold on to something, which I did (it was the kitchen counter) and bend down, crouching as far as possible, forcing my injured leg to bend.

This was novel. I stood taller after struggling to do this every morning for several months. Everybody noticed. In fact the security guard at the hospital where I volunteered asked if I had undergone surgery. I tried another gym where I did the aerobic classes. These classes all used therabands on one's legs. The thought behind this was to provide résistance to firm up the legs, as they were moved apart in scissor-like motion. I did that. I even asked an aerobic instructor if I could have some of that band so I could use the stuff at home because this resistance was more thorough than any weight I had ever used. This motion reintroduced the leg to my brain, or so I hoped.

My job at the bank meant I was on my feet a lot. The commercial loan servicing unit approved the loans before they were funded. Lots of dialogue existed between us and the lenders because documentation was never perfect at the time of funding, nor did our department see that the loan had sufficient approval to fund. Either of these situations resulted in waivers from the authorities received by way of fax, thus assuring the commercial loan customer would get his money. These situations made my day exciting.

I noticed I had stopped walking into walls so much. It was great! What a relief it was to realize that I could move without so much concentration.

In May of 1990 I decided to do a 5K race in the city which was sponsored by the bank. I had felt so sure that even though I hadn't run for 6 years, I was in good enough shape to endure the run. After 2 miles my leg muscle ripped so bad, I felt it never would heal. It was because of this running race that I realized that my brain had no idea where my leg was. Pain was constant, relentless and accompanied every move. For months no sign of healing materialized or at least the healing was so slow, I didn't notice. The therapist at the hospital where I sought advice on healing assured me nothing was written concerning how to go about curing such an injury. However, the pain eventually lessened using an ultra-sound vibrator.

I also asked that therapist, Karin, about head-injury to see if she knew any new therapies for improving my condition. She acknowledged that my recovery from the head trauma had been different but nothing had ever been ever written about this. When I told her how I had improved so dramatically in such a short time by doing the one-legged squat, she said people's reactions to recovery would be given only because people don't want to discourage; they want to be nice. So in effect my life was easier but since I was still so handicapped, nothing had really happened. Karin discouraged my hope that I could change how my body reacted to its surroundings. She also helped me prepare the article for ADVANCE, the magazine for Therapists.

ADVANCE for Therapists, May 20, 1991

My answer to this pain involved having a goal. I would go to the calendar and count 12 weeks from the date when I had began a certain theraband activity. I knew the body required 12 weeks to make a new muscle as a chiropractor had told me this years ago, so maybe nerves would work the same way. I told myself I would do the activity for a 12-week duration and after, if I hadn't noticed any progress, any lessening of the pain from that running injury, or any increased feeling, I could stop. It never occurred that there was no improvement in the condition so I just continued. At the time I was doing aerobics so I could honestly feel the subtle changes and improvements coming as a result of the theraband use. My aerobics instructor said I was incredible.

My dear friend, who eventually became the father of my child, called it "*a change in hegemony.*" What medicine needed was a change in hegemony if it was to embrace the work required in my recovery. "What is that?" I had asked. He replied he loved challenges when reading which required looking at a dictionary. As a doctor, he knew it was assumed the pains of my disorder never left. He saw my life as a miracle. I translated the statement "a change in hegemony" to mean that medicine believes the nervous system a person is born with has superior weight, force, importance, and influence over the body and that no other nerves can be made. Once the nervous system is gone, there's no living. Changing that belief is hard. My friend was a family physician who had never witnessed anyone working so hard in the gym until he saw me.

My friend the doctor had called me an angel. I used the new phrase he taught me *Change in Hegemony* as I wrote for "The Perspectives Network." I also wrote another article for a therapist's magazine ADVANCE. Both the articles made me feel as if I had accomplished something. I made the decision to learn what it was that my body was responding to and write about it so if someone else wanted to regain control, they would know what was done and how someone else did it. I had felt the theraband was so important to recovery along with the one-legged squat. It was so important to feel this control. I realized then the truth of having goals, faith, and determination. The article published in the therapist's magazine had at least one response. Patricia came from New York to visit me after reading the article. She had suffered an aneurism and was struggling to walk. She was very surprised to see I had so much difficulty. I guess I spoke in that article as if my condition were a thing of the past, showing I still lived in denial, although I was beginning to realize this condition could respond.

I did a few talks that year, one to a group of Brain Injury Survivors at a BIA conference and the other to a group of nursing students. The teacher there from Wayne State University told his students my recovery was unusual.

Here is where desire entered, the most vital of all requirements for this effort. I could finally see how much extra work it took me just to live and move. It would seem no-one else can take responsibility for this effort. I see therapists still very reluctant to give false hope. I was not happy with what I had but it became apparent that change could happen even if nobody could show the way. That neurologist from long ago had also told me that no one would ever care for me as much as me. It was my reality. That must have been the defining factor in my struggle to regain some normalcy in my life. I somehow got the ability to know how to look for improvement, yet not be overly hopeful and do whatever it took

How exactly was I to express my feelings that medicine/therapy could change and disability could be treated differently? The survivor should be taught the principles about their body that I was learning. Almost everyone close to me was in the medical profession. My mother owned and operated a temporary healthcare agency and my father did the accounts receivable for her business. My other younger brother was a Registered Nurse for a long time before becoming a Catholic priest, and my sister was an admired and sought after OB/GYN Doctor here in the area where I now live. How could I ever hope to get someone upset about the need for change when they had been taught it wasn't possible or relied totally on luck? My argument met the futility of the situation. I would prove them all wrong.

After a few years of this physical activity, I met two people who observed these changes happening in my life and encouraged me to write a book about it. That changed the way I felt about my life, The first person was Beth York, a co-worker at the bank where I worked. After I told her about my injury, she was amazed that my entire adult life had been spent so disabled. I explained to her that the doctors told me that they knew nothing to help and that I had been told it was all up to me. She felt it was not right that everything had to be so self-directed. She said that if someone were to see me today they wouldn't guess all that I had been through. I enjoyed her friendship

The second person was Don Rappaport, whom I met in 1996.Don taught music in Philadelphia at the time. He walked everywhere downtown, just like me. One day he gifted me with a poster of "Christina's World", a wonderful painting of a crippled girl in a field, by the late Andrew Wyeth. He said the determined look of Christina reminded him of me. Don died unexpectedly of natural causes in his apartment shortly after helping me write my first collection of memoirs. Beth got married and moved to North Carolina. So I lost my two best supporters not long after I had found them.

With my new found agility, I consciously began to add dance to my agenda. I remembered the advice of that physiatrist from twenty years ago. In Philadelphia, I lived behind a secured gate in Bainbridge Court and one of my neighbors in the court was going to a contra-dance on the north side of town. She invited me to accompany her.

CHAPTER 4

The path between you and your goal is seldom straight.

The dancing was a new experience for me in my post-accident life. My handicapped existence had made me quite self-centered and feeling very isolated. I began to open up with newfound friends from contra-dancing. The dancing community as a whole was and still is the most accepting, wonderful community I had ever experienced.

I met a man dancing. He called the morning after we met to invite me to lunch. I enjoyed this man paying extra attention to me and seeing someone different from work or the gym was a welcome change. I still felt so isolated and was sure that getting married was the route to happiness. Why not with this guy? Everyone in church and many co-workers had done the marriage route as opposed to being single. Room-mates were OK but marriage was definitely something I should do.

Turns out, I was wrong. Marriage wasn't something for me. My life with my husband in fact turned out to be little more than the subject for a trashy novel. I had greatly enjoyed dancing and the social activities that went with it but my new husband discouraged continuing this activity. We fought a great deal. Being with him was worse than being alone. The bank where I worked eventually merged with another. Our bank's way of doing business was lost. I never adjusted to the consolidation and remember groaning to myself; wishing I could be laid off. It so happened that in April of 1999 I got my wish.

So I was without a job and the lackluster relationship with my husband had quickly soured. It was a costly divorce, but it was not so costly to obtain the Absolution from the church. In the months following the layoff as I hurried to find new employment, I rekindled some old friendships and made a new one. In the divorce proceedings, the police felt I should contact another woman who had also been wrongfully treated by my husband. She had Parkinson's disease. I did meet with her on several occasions and we became friends. Her spastic and uncontrolled movement reminded me of how I must have appeared years ago. I shared with her the new exercises I had found and the new freedom of movement they imbued in me. However, I was still in denial. A mutual acquaintance thought I was crazy when he looked at me and heard my claims of moving more easily. Indeed, my claims were still based on self-delusion.

My sister said, "Congratulations! You're pregnant!". The child to be born was not my ex-husband's. Perhaps the inadequacy I was left with from the troubled marriage forced me into the arms of someone who had watched me at the gym for so long, my friend the doctor. Wasn't it

Paul in Romans, Chapter 7 who said "What I do I do not understand but I do not do what I want but I do what I hate… It is the sin which dwells in me" I couldn't imagine a worse punishment than being alone. Isolation is a punishment for those in jail not for the civil. I remember pleading with God how could he make me so awkward?? Even that husband I had laughed at my deformity If I couldn't even accept myself, how could I expect someone else to accept me? I just couldn't help but take advantage of my current situation with the doctor.

My dad pointed out to my very upright mother who would never approve of unwed sex that we would all adjust. He also told me to forgive my ex. My sister must have pointed out to my mom that I must be very lonely. She herself had two beautiful children. I was the godmother of the eldest. My mother insisted I come back to Michigan. I began to work for her business over the internet, joining other technology experts to develop a company website.

On Halloween of 2000, I moved from Philadelphia to Midland, Michigan. I was almost ready to give birth to what has become the greatest blessing of my lifetime. A co-worker at my mother's business at that time pointed out that birth is God's gift to woman. I found an apartment in Midland and prepared for the birth of my baby. My mother's sister came from London, Ontario to be the doula. I forget about the miraculous 12-week recovery time I had realized in Philadelphia and the joy of new ease in movement which could occur. My baby rightfully occupied my major energies.

In 2002 my mother reached retirement age. After she sold her business, I lost my job as technology specialist. I eventually worked with Michigan Rehabilitation Services(MRS) to begin my own business. I started my own business designing websites and I became very attracted to the network marketing industry. Network Marketing holds many positive attributes but two big negatives. You need to rearrange your whole life to become adjusted to life as a business-owner who has slight income at first and as an independent distributor, you need to buy untold amounts of the company's products. I've benefited greatly by attending and listening to some network marketing conferences. I've heard from the greats (people doing exceedingly well), and other motivational speakers. I always tried to glean what I can and these talks of inspiration and motivation got me dreaming and planning again. It also made me realize the enormity of the problem.

In 2004 I attended a conference at the Holiday Inn sponsored by MRS. I met a man who had just recovered from a stroke and his stories of life after a stroke were amusing. His journey sounded somewhat similar to mine. Si Fu Chung's attitude and recovery had been so great that the MidMichigan hospital sought him as a mentor for other stroke patients. I rode my bike to visit him at his karate school every two weeks. He gave me several suggestions on building my body.

I started lifting a soup can in front of a mirror. As I attempted Si Fu Chung's suggested leg strengthening exercises, one man at the gym commented that I was becoming an almost normal person. My right leg was strengthening so that it was better able to support my right torso and I was beginning to untwist. I stopped seeing Si-Fu when I realized it was only time which could heal my wounds. Si-Fu had also said he didn't know if his techniques could help the kink which had developed in my sternum. Our meeting was very crucial as he held the same belief about disability that I had. Any situation can be improved if you're willing to do the work.

A few years back I held the position of lunchroom assistant in the school where my daughter attends. One day, the lunchroom was rearranged to accommodate a funeral for a veteran. One of the funeral attendees remarked to me something about quality of life for some of the veterans returning from Iraq or Afghanistan. He questioned whether it was worth it. He felt some of the veterans didn't have too much of a life to return to. I agree with him. That is a difficult life until the survivor can figure out certain things. I see these guys on certain TV specials and I'm always reminded of how lucky I am.

Today I spend at least an hour a day at the local gym very mindful of all the mobility problems which can arise from any number of circumstances. The gym is the great equalizer. People in all states of life come there. It is there I learned how physical conditions can be made manageable. I am also reminded of another network marketing mantra which helped me in my struggle. "The definition of insanity is doing the same thing over and over again, and expecting different results." I see people at the gym doing things so dutifully, over and over again, and wish all could receive the guidance I've been given.

As a small business owner, it is easy to see the impact of certain things going on around town. I have been a member of the Chamber of Commerce for years and nothing comes close to the impact of a certain minor league baseball team. In 2007, the Dow Chemical Corporation purchased the Great Lakes Loons. In Major League Baseball,(the MLB) the Loons feed the L.A. Dodgers and are the A-division baseball team. Starting in June of 2007, I began to notice I was working alongside these guys. That year I remember talking to the trainer and telling him how lucky we were in Midland to have the Loons here. The team didn't fare that well that year but business sure improved. Hotels sprang up around the city, businesses in general tried to upgrade themselves. The entire downtown landscape changed as old "eyesores" houses were demolished and new buildings replaced them. No one likes to see business failure so the very fact that the Loons are thriving here and contribute so much to our economy is a gift.

My second year working alongside the Loons, I noticed this trainer did things a little differently than the athletic trainer of the first year. This guy employed the pulley along with other methods of strength training where the body resists itself. I became convinced the move he was doing would help me so I asked him how he did it. He was more than happy to show me his move which in essence involved moving the pulley from above his head down to his leg while standing on one leg. I couldn't do it. He then modified his routine so that I could do it. I was just bending over and holding on to a 10 pound weight. This developed my hamstrings. By the end of the summer two months later, sufficient muscle had developed so I could attempt the one-legged maneuver on the pulley.

I also used the Smith machine, a piece of equipment just purchased by the community center. Normally it provides users support in squat-like activities. I watched someone using it and became convinced her move could help me. I just stood in one place raising myself up and down on my toe. I learned to put the bar on my shoulder so that my entire foot could feel the resistance. As I did this calf raise I was reminded that I had been told by a weight trainer years ago that this was the most difficult muscle to reach, as you use it every day. This was correct, it was a difficult muscle to reach, but for a different reason. I don't think sitting and trying to use the calf raise machine as he had suggested would have caused enough resistance to develop this muscle. The Smith machine allowed my entire leg to get in the action. I was so excited to feel my calf. I also remember one of the Loon's stars of that year telling me that I was his hero. He was a great athlete. I was so touched by that comment. All the negative, self-doubting thoughts changed again with his comment and my forgotten commitment about writing was rekindled.

The next year one of the sluggers had a higher on-base percentage than anyone in the Loon's brief history so this earned his picture being placed on the team's website. I immediately recognized him when I saw him later that morning at the gym and called out to him. We became friends and later that summer he assured me somebody would care about my efforts. Fighting against myself had become sort of a battle. I was ready to again begin to fight. I wonder why it took me so long to realize I needed to fight? Was it that I never imagined these moves which require contemplation could help?

CHAPTER 5

The Lord replied: "My precious, precious child I would never leave you at your times of trial and suffering. When you see only one set of footprints, it was then that I carried you."

From Footprints, Author:
Guideposts Magazine

In November of 2008, after another visit with a counselor at MRS, I prepared to re-enter the workforce. She suggested that I first visit a chiropractor. Remembering the trips to the chiropractor made while in high school, I was skeptical. That chiropractor had done nothing except to insert a lift in the right shoe and place electrodes on my leg for 20 minute sessions. Neither suggestion led to any recovery. But by now my back and neck were really sore, my arms tingled periodically and I couldn't understand why. So I took her suggestion. This chiropractor was different. He ascribed to the NUCCA (National Upper Cervical Chiropractic Association) practice. The visit once again reminded me of the uniqueness of my circumstance. After x-rays and scanning my back, he was amazed by what he found during that first evaluation. He was surprised I could even walk with such bodily distortion.

His very technical analysis read that my right leg was ¼ inch functionally shorter than my left, my right hip was one degree lower than my left and my right shoulder was two degrees behind that of my left shoulder. The x-ray showed a five-degree to the right misalignment of the C-1 vertebrae and a four degree posterior rotation of the underlying vertebrae.

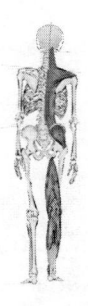

Illustration courtesy of www.chirocorrection.com

The underlying vertebrae had rotated into the left frontal plane. My body had done this to cope with demands for muscle support during movement throughout the years. In other words I was pretty twisted up and I limped due to the functional discrepancy. I say functional because these symptoms, termed cervical syndrome symptoms, corrected and the 1/4 inch difference in my leg stance which caused the limp disappeared as I turned my head in either direction. The goal of my therapy would be to unwind the torso and maintain that corrected posture for a sustained period.

Going to his therapy did help straighten my torso. Never again did the vertebrae go back to its 5-degree misalignment but another problem emerged. A few areas in my right leg still lacked strength, despite the years I had tried to use weight machines, free weights and therabands. My right arm still hung from its socket as if it were not my own. The chiropractor had no suggestion regarding acquiring strength in either my arm or my leg but my MRS counselor suggested I try more therapy. Such C-1 vertebrae dislocation as I had exhibited ruptures nerve pathways but now that the distortion of the vertebrae was less maybe my leg and my arm would now respond to some new therapy suggestions.

Julie, the therapist, accompanied me as I exercised and encouraged me in how to perform stretches along with common sense things like my engaging lower abdomen in exercise and breathing. I was there to learn the latest way to gain arm strength.

I left therapy armed with a stack of pictures where people use therabands in different ways and lift light 2 pound weights or a soup can to develop the wrist. She also encouraged concentration while engaging in activities. This thought had been consistent throughout my long therapy, as I even remember being told the same 34 years ago in Detroit.

I asked about strengthening the leg. I still had dreams of a day when people would not stare at my limp. Almost in disbelief, she wondered out loud how my body would respond if my right leg were to get stronger. The compensation in my body made her think I did not need further recovery in that leg. The pain in my knee told me otherwise, and this had become ever more uncomfortable with the cervical syndrome correction as noted above. Julie's suggestion was to just stand still on one leg.

For the next few months I stood on one leg every chance I could. I stood on one leg at the bus depot holding on to the suitcase containing my Easter garb to visit my aunt, the same aunt who was mid-wife at Annie's birth. I stood on one leg holding on to the walls surrounding the stairwell as I listened to the Loon's baseball games blaring out of the basement radio. Later that summer at the gym I began standing on the top of a rubber half-circle ball(termed a bosu ball)and rolling it under my foot front-to-back while holding on to something. According to the chiropractor, this activity would increase proprioception or the body's ability to sense its position in space, another thing which was destroyed in the injury.

Later in July, after approximately 12 weeks of these leg strengthening techniques, I realized true leg strength did return. I remember being congratulated by my mother and the Loon's trainer as well as a few Loons' players. So I began doing tricep dips, another exercise I've watched others complete where the body resists itself. I did the exercise to see if my arm would respond to its own resistance like my leg did.

It did. It was the resistance which re-introduced my arm to my brain. The square box on which I propped my hands was a foot high and I watched constantly in the mirror to assure my right arm would mimic the left. My neck and shoulders were in the chin-locked position while I pushed up and then returned to the floor. Resistance came from that motion.

A few years back, I remember reading in a Newsweek magazine about how stroke patients regained use of their arm just by using it so I had tried to actively use my arm for at least 7 years. I came to the conclusion my arm would never be the same. After the birth of my baby I had overextended my left arm and required a carpal-tunnel release surgery. The orthopedic doctor had told me I would never again be able to lift any significant weight. He also told me I needed a new right knee. My arm had hurt constantly since that surgery until I did this tricep dip exercise. The exercise improved both arms, better than I could have ever imagined possible.

It was in the gym where I showed yet another therapist the dip exercise that was working on my arm. I remember thinking she might be interested since her patient was displaying many of the symptoms I had felt for so long. After watching me complete the exercise she just gasped and remarked that it must be difficult. She was sure it might strengthen the triceps. Well yes, it would strengthen my triceps along with my hands, my shoulders and probably the forearms not to mention improving the circulation of the entire arm. The chiropractor suggested that because the dip required at least 3 muscles all working together at the same time, it was a superior motion to the isolation techniques available in gyms or therapy.

As mentioned in the prior chapter, I've tried to make it in the business world and have been greeted with various levels of success. I am familiar with therapy sessions and would grade my own experience as questionable. I must have exhibited symptoms out of the ordinary, but I knew what my goal was. I'm not sure of what all the therapy did if anything. Using the same standards which businesses use to remain in existence or "survival of the fittest," would I again pay for all that? Maybe yes. Maybe no. Therapy was able to get me functional but anything beyond that I owed to my resolution. Just like that neurologist had predicted. No amount of concentration could have ever done what those one legged squats or the tricep dips did. So much money went into my recovery and did so little good. I was better off on my own listening to my body or at a good gym where so many tools and posters are to assist in the fight. This is what every disabled person deserves to hear.

I asked Julie why she felt so many faced with nerve loss choose the wheel chair or even the cane. She said she believed it was fear. Yes, moving without consciousness of a body part is frightening but I've learned one's body can adapt. Muscles which the brain does recognize can compensate for those muscles which have been disabled by brain injury. Eventually, new nerve pathways can be forged to get the proper muscles to function again normally if one can just learn how to properly exercise his body. The real trouble was that no one ever knew how to show me. But I learned. Enduring my life without the benefit of those forged nerve paths made me more patient, more empathetic and more determined. It also has me thinking about others caught in that predicament, where walking is difficult because no nerve feeling comes from that half of the body to tell the brain it is still there. Although my solution came from unexpected sources like a cast worn when I broke my foot the first summer after the injury, a karate instructor back in Philadelphia or Dr. John and his miraculous chiropractic techniques, I got the help I needed. We can and should give this sort of beneficial help to those in need. True: the body is a prison, but it is also a wondrous thing if it can be worked properly. Look at all my body did, how it twisted in the effort when the muscles stopped receiving proper nerve signals from the brain.

It is only human to want to have certain actions occur when the brain gives orders. It is a divine right to want to look human. Something happens to make the survivor of this injury look different., and he may not be able to move. Current treatment is inadequate. Where the suggested therapy and subsequent living may be more difficult than the work required to re-establish the body, the bridge of ignorance must be crossed. Medicine and therapy can now save and they should give more authoritative solutions when it comes to matters of the brain and existing in this body. I found living without conditioned nerves to be a deplorable state, but it was one that could be changed. A change in hegemony might not be a bad idea. I wonder today what would happen if knowing what I know now, I could do it again.

Remember the old adage promoted in the network marketing industry. "Facts bore, stories sell." I remember feverishly pacing up and down the backyard many summers following the injury. I had been told a story about a girl who recovered from an injury similar to mine by holding a glass of water and walking. She recovered so well she was able to volunteer for army duty. This story kept my hopes alive. It would appear to me that we can now do the same.

CHAPTER 6

Exercise adds years to your life and life to your years.

*T*he job of therapy is to point to a home program. Of course you want to be functional after an experience such as I had. I did not mean to sound so negative when I questioned their purpose. I just was never satisfied with the results. Therapy ended speculation that weights would help my leg to redevelop. I know they did the best they could with the knowledge they had at the time. I didn't remember my non-compliant behavior in therapy as a teenager until I started using the weights and feeling the difference when I was preparing writings back in Philadelphia. The book got mixed reviews and eventually publishers and editors pointed to the relatively small percentage of people who are affected. I realized my tale to encourage society was just not worth it. I was still extremely disabled and had not yet realized the consequence that my long-term commitment would have.

Dancing was one of the first activities I started when I first moved to Midland in 2000. I dance the 2nd and 4th Saturday of each month with the Midland Traditional Dancers. The physical fitness recently gained contributes to the experience and helps to participate in the dances. But such fitness is not necessary. I've received so much awareness from attending these dances and could not have made this progress in my physical fitness if fitness were a requirement. I see all kinds of people with physical disorder (Parkinson's, stroke victims, cerebral palsy, muscular dystrophy among others) on the dance floor and am reminded that so many of these disorders could benefit from greater awareness.

Earlier in the year, I had volunteered at the concession stand to earn money for my church at a Loon's playoff game. Those boys did so well their third year and it was a very tight game. The Loons were not ahead once in the game. They came from behind to tie it with a 3-run homerun in the bottom of the ninth by a player who had shaken my hand earlier in the summer to congratulate me for the victory in my leg strength, my victory over cervical syndrome. I remember shouting in my active-spectator voice "Come on Jaime, we need a home run." First and second were filled with runners and even I had my doubts as to the decision of the game. Jaime missed the first few pitches but on what would otherwise have been the final out of the game, he hit a deep right field home run. There was no doubt about it: in extra innings the Loons managed to load the bases and then score again. I did not get home that night until 11:45pm. It was quite exciting.

No one can give the exact cause to this successful homerun. However, just as in the above example, the hearing of my comment could have prompted the young athlete to increase his focus, so does the survivor need a goal and increased focus to bring his limbs into his brain's awareness. He needs to work at this awareness between his brain and his body. He can and he should.   He can exercise with purpose.

Earlier in that game, back in the concession stand, I felt a slight disappointment for being placed in the 3rd base side concession instead of the 1st base side, where my church St. Brigid normally serves. On the first-base side, the Loons players with the night off normally frequent at snack time and I wished to tell the players how impressive they had been in the playoffs thus far, but as the story goes, the supervisor of the stand on the 3rd base side was none other than Dan. He is the brother of John, the boy whom I mentioned at the beginning of the story as being with me the night of the injury. Dan was one of the others who had gone seeking to rouse someone for assistance after the car had struck me. He said he was surprised to see me. He would not have thought that I would look so well and he didn't know such a thing was possible. He commented "Boy, that 30 years made such a difference." I thought to myself it has been 33 almost 34 years, but who's counting anymore.

Earlier in the summer I was at Tiger Stadium for a "Green Day". The Multi-Level Marketing (MLM) company I represented partnered with the Tigers by sponsoring the "Green" weekend. The first ten thousand fans had been promised a shopping bag. Here I was at the main gate passing out these bags, overwhelmed a little because the Tiger's Management expected the bags to be stuffed with a flyer from my company. They had given us volunteers little time to accomplish this task. I stood there against a sell-out crowd , passing out the "Go Green" bags, only half my bags had the desired flyer inside. With the force of the crowd it was difficult just to remove the bags from the boxes, let alone to stuff them all with the flyer.

A few persons in wheel chairs and a few people using canes came in that day. One fan with a cane caught my attention because he was so young, probably his mid 20's. He self-effaced himself by mumbling about being crippled as he attempted to keep up with his friends. He had the same rendered inoperative look I know I had for years. I bet he had wings on his heart too. If someone were to show him, he would again be able to work at his recovery.

Besides using and selling the cleaning products made by this MLM company, I've learned so many advantages to being green. Most products work with greater efficacy than those with chemicals. My customers appreciate the non-chemical atmosphere and brilliant cleaning properties these products deliver. Midland's called "chemical city" so it's going to take some visionary thinking to compete with the Chemical giants in this city. Research shows some 20 toxic chemicals exist in a baby's umbilical cord at birth. I know there is such a thing as "safe use" for chemicals but look at what they do. Many destroy our environment and can cause cancer, so they can eventually destroy us. Companies have no obligation to point out long-term effects. This does not mention that the chemical production makes our community a key target for terrorist activity.

I've also learned that a requirement for success in any MLM company is to believe in the product so when I learned I was getting a business as I bought my water machine I realized I had a story. I remember the pain in my knees caused as the joints rubbed together and the sudden relief I felt when I began hydrating my body by drinking this water in sufficient amounts. I would have done anything to relieve the pain and avoid the knee replacement surgery the doctor felt should occur. I was taking unsafe doses of pain reliever. After a few days of drinking this water, I could stop taking the pain relievers, cold turkey.

When told of the cost of this machine, along with the descent of its maker,(a Japanese man created this water technology) I had no doubt as to the worth of this investment. Remembering that Karate instructor in Philadelphia who instructed me in the one-legged squat and now this water technology, I was left believing the Orientals must be light years ahead of us Americans in studying the body. My sponsor's sponsor in this company also showed similar results with his knees, as he was and continues to be an avid runner. There are also numerous health benefits to drinking this ionized water. When questioned as to the cost, he merely replies that being sick is expensive too.

I now try to live with "passion," a phrase coined by my favorite Passionist priest Cedric Pisegna. I met him as he gave a mission at St Brigid earlier in the summer. His writings, TV programs, missions and retreats exemplify the approach I have strived for in my life. His instructions about taking responsibility for your own actions and to "activate your faith" were important thoughts which helped me realize that I approached life or at least had tried to with the same gusto. His saying that the devil won't know what to do with you when you begin to activate your faith made me laugh and was my favorite.

I also worry about our country, and whether it's going in the right direction. I know that the current thought about embryonic stem-cell research and cloning as being a solution to nerve damage is in all likelihood incorrect. Don't they see all the sin? After suffering nerve loss and then recovering I know, it is more effective not to mention cheaper to bring that joint or body part into the sufferer's brain awareness and then using strength and conditioning techniques. I've learned for any change, the key is to imagine it. How would that pill ever work? It is a disservice to bring false hopes to those in need. Don't we play gods when we manufacture and destroy life?

My mother questioned me as to why I would object to such research when I could receive the potential benefit. Well I suppose stem cell research can find something to speed up the recovery time but it will come from the body's own stem cells or adult stem cells and not from embryonic or that which is made just to destroy. The chief mechanism regarding embryonic research starts with a practice the Church condemns. The Catholic Church gives adequate guidance regarding the birth of a child and anything else is wrong. The resulting situation is not fair to the child.

I read *Dreams of My Father* with great interest and could see God's touch in Obama's life. I'm just not sure he does. Is going against the church on so many issues going to lead to our nation's demise? I learned God is very real. I will be forever changed. You can't have sin in one area of your life and expect victory in another.

The content of my book would suggest a higher being exists but that was not the intent of my writing this book. God has been with me since day one when He was the bright light shining in my unconscious state. Hopefully, a shift in treatment can occur and people will realize there is much they can do, even when they can't move on their own. What you need is desire. The thing I lost, I've found again. I lost my life, but now I've reclaimed it.

EPILOGUE

Blessed are the clean of heart, for they will see God.
Matthew 5, 8

Since the writing and sharing of these thoughts on the work in my recovery, a few glaring omissions have been brought to my attention which I need to clarify. When exactly did emotional acceptance come and when did I realize I needed to work?

I'm not sure acceptance ever did or will come. It's a lot of deal with and the condition can respond to certain activity. Satisfaction has come in achieving the level of awareness I now have. However, I still get disturbed by people's stares and grimace as I see myself in the mirror of a changing room at a clothing store. But I've learned that it is this denial which is my friend and keeps me working. On the next point, I think I always worked in my therapy. The problem was just that it focused on optimizing the present, subsequently leading to further alienation between me and my body whereas I had always focused on the future. I dreamed about what would help my body, hoping therapy's suggestions could lead me to a pre-injury status. Clearly this was not the case. People who receive help for their injured body are the only ones who can change the situation they are in. It is a tragedy and they are the ones being exploited because the people who seek to help really can't or don't know how to instruct.

For example of this, I need tell you that I followed the advice for the marketing of this book and I put out the keywords "LIVING WITH PARALYSIS" on a popular search engine just to see who I might want to establish an internet relationship with. Less than an hour had passed when I received a call from a lawyer, wanting to sue. I told him "No, I didn't want to sue. I just wanted to see if anybody would be interested in corresponding with someone who had survived such tragedy and then beat the odds."

But I had already found such an individual to correspond with and I had just forgotten. Earlier in the summer, .I had emailed an earlier version of this story to my brother the priest, suggesting his friend read my story and find a Chiropractor specializing in NUCCA. Albert is now the rector of the St. Mary's Cathedral in Austin., TX and he had read the memoirs I had written in Philadelphia so he knew of my interest in nerves. When one of his parishioners had spinal injuries, he came to Father Albert for spiritual counseling, An abscess in this man's back led to spinal surgery and this subsequently meant destruction of nerve endings in specific parts of his legs and toes. I remember laughing to myself when this injured man had first started emailing me and told me of his dilemma. To quote him "I realized very early on in this process that I was on my own when I spent 2 useless weeks at a rehab center. Their work week was Monday - Friday noon, and

I got about 2 hours a day of training. The other 21+ spent wasting my time in my room. Just last week I challenged my therapist to put on paper the things I need to do to walk again, and give me a time-line. He was a bit perplexed, but did as I asked. I took my first two baby steps unaided on Friday." and "Little was I aware of the nerve's importance in walking and balance. So whilst at the gym, a trainer with experience grabbed me and took me to the training area which uses all of the therabands you had mentioned."

The survivor NEEDS to get angry with his circumstances, just like this man with SCI did. At the facility where I work out, a therapist from Special Tree Rehabilitation Center had noticed me working and I had noticed her trying to help an injured man in a wheel chair. Special Tree is a Neuro Skills Center here in Midland and after a brief introduction of myself to this therapist and a short life history, I ended up emailing her an earlier version of this story. She asked me to speak to their support group.

When I spoke to that group, I had told them, "there are so many opportunities you will miss out on because of your physical state and if you can't get angry with that, there isn't another option. I'll be 50 on my next birthday and I had the injury at 15. It never got any easier until I took control. The only thing which could truly direct me in my fight against hemi-paralysis was the pain felt from improper or inadequate exercise while living in a body with inadequate musculature due to nerve disorder". That isn't right. I said, "I feel the government had been outstanding in support of the disabled in the passing of the "Americans With Disabilities Act" and the subsequent support of it." I told them about sending Mr. Obama an earlier version of this book because I had heard him call for papers call for papers when speaking to a group of disabled veterans. I had stated in that paper that my therapy had been a dismal failure and I wouldn't pay for it again if given the option. I had also mentioned that developing a pill as a substitute for the effort of rehabilitation was a mistake and a disservice to the disabled. It would lead to distasteful hope mongering. He wrote me back thanking me for sharing my story and that he gets lots of correspondence from his public.

But then he funded additional embryonic stem-cell research....what in my story did he not understand? Did he read it all? I know it said *change in hegemony*. He must not have understood and I suspect many people don't understand. A few days prior to this funding decision, one of the worst environmental tragedies on record, the Gulf Coast Oil Spill happened. I suspect this was a scourge from the Almighty. I remember PBS's coverage of Mr. Obama earlier that spring when he said God did not belong in issues of science. What? God is the author of science. I suspect that he did not approve of this new kind of research. It's all because of the actions in this and many other sinful, amoral policies where the government now goes against the church. The Obama administration's inadequate response to this crisis leaves me with little question, although it's true, it is only speculation that the two could be related. His views leave me puzzled and hoping for change. And America does seem to want a pill for every ailment.

In the summer of 2010, my mother sent me another book, *Going Rogue* by Sarah Palin. I'm impressed, because she represents the change the US needs. I'm impressed with her sincerity, her candor and above all her ability to bring one of the most corrupt business' in our times to its knees. The book reviews her life and her eventual rise to the Vice-Presidential nomination a few years back. She would never take such an anti-life stance in moral issues. She is the true advocate for change. She has a good handle on life and I certainly hope her disdain for the media doesn't end her public service career.

In her book she shares a situation where her doctor told her that her child would have Down's syndrome. Her acceptance of this child is admirable and a situation I can speak to. Children born with the extra chromosome can do very well in this life if given the proper encouragement and treatment. Just as my body has improved with proper activity, so can her son's. She needs to help her son to engage in or encourage him to engage in a few of the things I've suggested in this book. I suspect these activities can help anyone struggling to get control over their body. My daughter now dances and in the dance company's performance a few years back were at least two young performers with disabilities. (One teenage girl had Down's syndrome and another little boy had a rare nerve disorder) They both performed wonderfully. Physical fitness can improve anyone's experience of life. Having my daughter and caring for her had to be the most important factor for getting me to realize this important fact about fitness. I wanted my daughter to have a good role model in life and to be proud to grow up beside someone who didn't make excuses, who didn't take the path of least resistance or who wouldn't settle for mediocrity and bend in her beliefs.

I also told the audience at Special Tree that night I spoke to the survivor's group that since writing President Obama I took back my view that therapy was a dismal failure. The therapy did get me working. I am now engaging in intensive calf raises on both legs and isolation techniques of toe raises on the right leg with help of leaning against a huge rubber ball, hoping that by week 12 of proper nerve resistance my gait will be steadier.

One lady from the support group asked "Well, what does work?" I told her of these new exercises with the ball and I had also earlier demonstrated to the group the one legged squat. I had said answers to my problem came from nowhere of real importance to me at the time. I think it is an area which needs more trial. Anyone who wants to move after disabling conditions happen should learn of this success, visit a NUCCA chiropractor, learn the proper activities to get similar results in their situation, and decide for themselves whether or not they're up to the activity or could be. The alternative of living life in a wheelchair and becoming dependant on others for everything is difficult. For me, it was unacceptable. This is an incredibly unfortunate circumstance where the survivor needs to put his foot down and say enough is enough. He needs to be empowered.

In concluding my talk that night I compared humans to the flowers in my garden. Gardening is one of my new passions. I had told the group how I had purchased a few flats of petunias and impatiens in support of my neighbor boy's pre-school. The flowers had arrived much too early in the season to be put out in the chilly Michigan spring so I had put them in the garage where they were somewhat protected even though there was no sunlight or water. Some of them had died but I said about 90% of these flowers had survived the garage experience. As of that morning, they were blooming again.

I had also received a poinsettia plant from my church last Christmas. I researched on the internet how to get this plant to bloom again. Among other things, the article suggested cutting the limbs to four inches, placing the plant in direct sunlight and looking for new signs of life. I was happy to report this plant now had new sprigs of life. I told the group we're just like the plants. Humans can suffer injury and pain but with perseverance, trying new things and hard work new life can happen. We just have to know how to look for it.

We Are Many Parts

We are many parts, we are all one body.
And the gifts we have we are given to share.
May the Spirit of love, make us one indeed.
One, the love that we share; one, our hope in despair,
one, the cross that we bear.

Marty Haugen
© 1986 GIA Publications

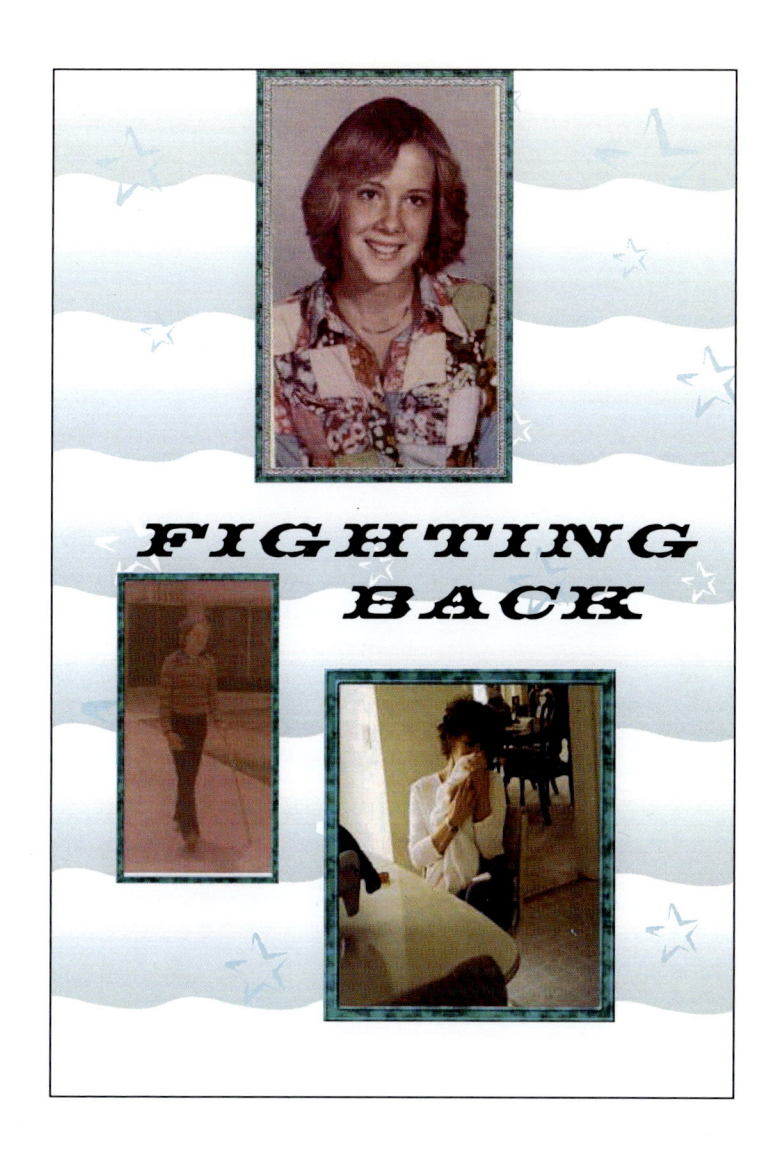

FIGHTING BACK

MARY ELIZABETH LAFORET

Anne LaForet

Dean · Black
School of Performing Arts
2010

FIGHTING BACK

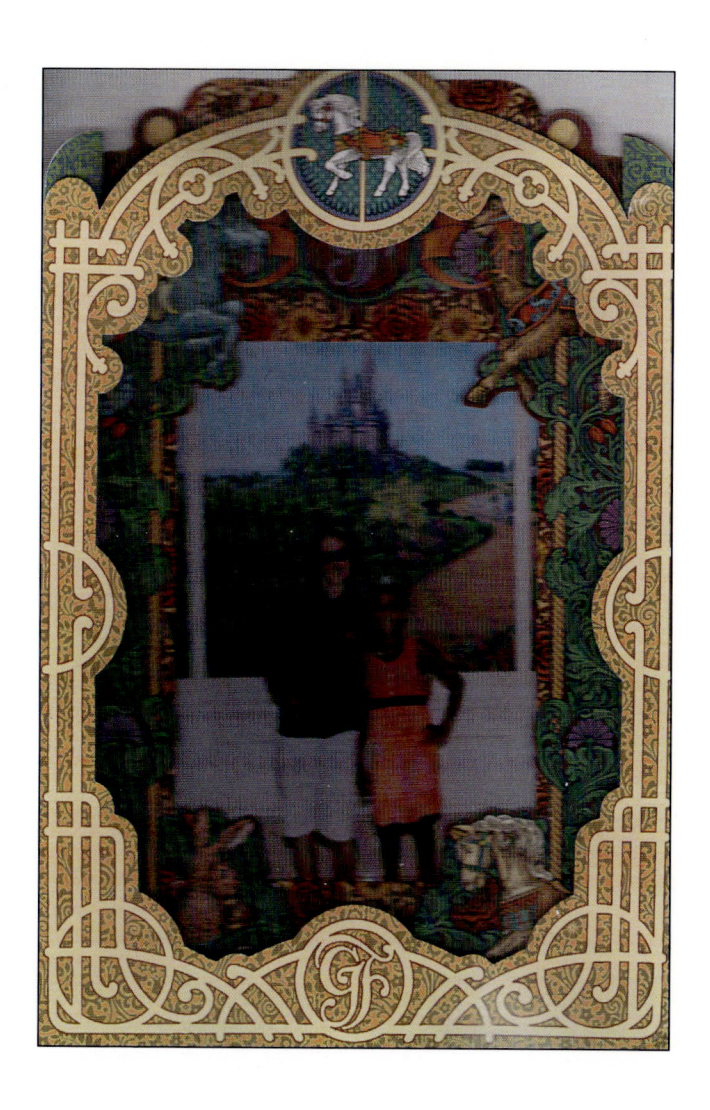